Have you noticed that there are a lot of incompetent people in the world? Personally, I've been incompetent at virtually every job I've ever had. Yet somehow I always managed to get paid. Sometimes I even got awards.

As far as I can tell, acting like you know what you're doing is just as profitable as knowing what you're doing, and it's a lot less work. Attitude succeeds where experience and skill dare not venture.

That's the theory behind this book. You'll see examples of Dogbert prospering by using little more than a total disdain for the intelligence of all human beings. It worked for him, it can work for you, and it will work for me if you buy this book.

S. Adams

ISBN: 0-8362-2196-6

YOU DON'T NEED EXPERIENCE IF YOU'VE GOT ATTITUDE

A DILBERT™ BOOK
BY
SCOTT ADAMS

ANDREWS and McMEEL
A UNIVERSAL PRESS SYNDICATE COMPANY
KANSAS CITY

DOGBERT'S TASK FORCE

I'M SURE THAT YOU ALL HAVE A COMMON VISION ABOUT THIS PROJECT...

SPECIFICALLY, YOU THINK IT WILL LOOK GOOD ON YOUR RESUMES WHILE BEING TOO FUTURISTIC TO GENERATE ANY REAL WORK.

MOTHER LODE

I WILL BE CHAIRMAN OF THE BOARD AND OWN 99% OF THE COMPANY. YOU WILL WORK FOR FREE AND WASH MY CAR TWICE A WEEK.

CAN I MOW YOUR LAWN INSTEAD OF WASHING YOUR CAR?

YOU'RE A TOUGH BARGAINER, BUT I PREFER MULTIMEDIA DEVELOPERS FOR MY GARDENING NEEDS.

HERE'S A PICTURE OF YOU LIVING
IN A DUMPSTER IN TWENTY YEARS.

DOGBERT:
FINANCIAL
ADVISOR

THIS IS
DOGBERT'S
HEADHUNTING
SERVICE.

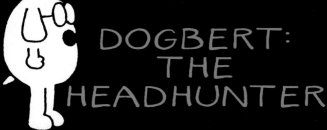

DOGBERT:
THE
HEADHUNTER

YOUR COMMERCIALS SHOULD COMPARE YOUR <u>BEST</u> ASSETS TO THE COMPETITION'S <u>WORST</u>.

DOGBERT'S AD AGENCY

ACCORDING TO MY ONLINE DATABASE, OUR PRODUCT ISN'T COMPATIBLE WITH YOUR COMPUTER.

DOGBERT'S TECH SUPPORT

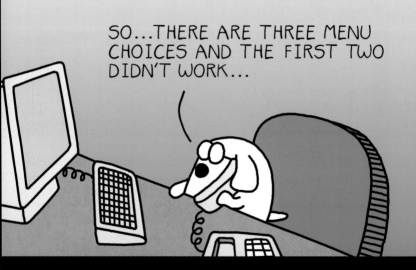

I INSERT THE VIDEO TAPE ... THEN I SET THE TIMER FOR NINETY MINUTES...

DOES ANYBODY KNOW WHY IT ISN'T WORKING?
THE FOOL! IT'S BETA!

MANY OF YOU COME TO MY MANAGEMENT SEMINAR AS OPTIMISTIC, CREATIVE, CLEAR-SPEAKING INDIVIDUALS.

DOGBERT'S SEMINAR ON MANAGEMENT ZOMBIES

BUT WITH HARD WORK, YOU CAN BECOME JARGON-SPEWING CORPORATE ZOMBIES, LIKE CARL HERE.

I WANT TO DIALOGUE WITH YOU ABOUT UTILIZING RESOURCES.

GOOD BOY! HERE'S A DONUT.

TALK TO
ME, BABE!